SHARPEN YOUR
VERBAL
SKILLS

SHARPEN YOUR

VERBAL SKILLS

PEARL U. ANUKU

iUniverse, Inc.
Bloomington

Sharpen Your Verbal Skills

iUniverse books may be ordered through booksellers or by contacting:

iUniverse
1663 Liberty Drive
Bloomington, IN 47403
www.iuniverse.com
1-800-Authors (1-800-288-4677)

ISBN: 978-1-4759-8442-2 (sc)
ISBN: 978-1-4759-8443-9 (ebk)

Library of Congress Control Number: 2013907788

Printed in the United States of America

iUniverse rev. date: 06/04/2013

CONTENTS

This book is dedicated to my late parents, Mr. Martin Ifeonukwu Etuokwu and Mrs. Roseline Uche Etuokwu, for being there for me during their lifetime.

"Talent alone cannot make a writer. There must be a man behind the book; a personality which, by birth and quality, is pledged to the doctrines there set forth, and which exists to see and state things so, and not otherwise."

—Ralph Waldo Emerson

PREFACE

Most people find it difficult to express themselves in English, especially in the area of subject-verb agreement. This is because they do not know the fundamentals of this topic; that is, matching a singular subject with a singular verb and a plural subject with a plural verb. It is against this backdrop that *Sharpen Your Verbal Skills* is specifically designed.

Indeed, this book will be of immense benefit to pupils in primary schools, students in secondary and higher education, and the general public.

ACKNOWLEDGEMENTS

I appreciate my husband, Walter Anuku, and our children Samuel, Israel, and Jesse for their unreserved love and understanding.

Also, worthy of note is the grace of God, which saw me through the writing process.

LIST OF ABBREVIATIONS AND SIGNS USED

PP—prepositional phrase
PS—plural subject
PV—plural verb
SS—singular subject
SS1—singular subject (first)
SS2—singular subject (second)
SS3—singular subject (third)
SV—singular verb
=—equal to
+—plus

CHAPTER 1

DEFINITION OF TERMS

Sentence
Verb
Subject

Sentence

"A set of words expressing a statement, a question, or an order, usually containing a subject and a verb" (*Oxford Advanced Learner's Dictionary*, 2005: 1331).

Verb

"A word used to indicate the occurrence of or performance of an action" (*The New Shorter Oxford English Dictionary*, 1993: 3562).

Subject

"A word or phrase in a sentence indicating who or what performs the action of a verb" (*Oxford Canadian Dictionary of Current English*, 2005: 843).

From the above definitions, it is obvious that a sentence is complete only when there is a combination of a subject and a verb. While the verb "expresses" the action, the subject "does" the action. Here are some examples:

Sentence 1:   A chorister sings.

Subject + Verb

Sentence 2:   The girl is wild.

Subject + Verb

Sentence 3:   My father is a genius.
           ↑ ↑
          Subject + Verb

Sentence 4:   This car is very expensive.
           ↑ ↑
          Subject + Verb

Sentence 5:   The children are hungry.
           ↑   ↑
          Subject + Verb

Sentence 6:   Those students are very intelligent.
           ↑   ↑
          Subject + Verb

Sentence 7:   The women are dancing.
           ↑ ↑
          Subject + Verb

Sentence 8:   The man is jogging.
           ↑ ↑
          Subject + Verb

Sentence 9:   My sister is an engineer.
           ↑ ↑
          Subject + Verb

Sentence 10:   God is faithful.
         ↑ ↑
       Subject + Verb

In view of the above examples, it is clear that a sentence without a subject and a verb is like the alphabet without its letters or a car without an engine.

CHAPTER 2

SUBJECT-VERB AGREEMENT RULE

WHAT IS AGREEMENT?

Agreement is "the condition of having the same number, gender, case, or person" (*The Canadian Oxford Dictionary*, 1998: 24).

In line with the above definition, subject-verb agreement is the matching of subject and verb according to person and number. This means that if the subject of a sentence is singular, the verb must be singular (singular subject + singular verb), and if the subject is plural, the verb must also be plural (plural subject + plural verb).

APPROACH

Step 1:   Ensure that you know what the subject is.

Step 2:   Find out whether the subject is singular or plural.

Step 3:   Be able to identify a singular or plural verb.

Step 4:   Match a singular subject with a singular verb and a plural subject with a plural verb.

For clarity, below is a table that shows persons and their singular and plural formations.

Persons	Singular	Plural
First person	I	We
Second person	You	You
Third person	He, She, It	They

Before explaining the above table, it is important to note the following points.

-s   -es

🔸 Verbs that have "-s" or "-es" endings are singular and, therefore, require singular subjects.

| He   She   It |

🔸 Verbs in the present tense for third-person singular subjects (he, she, it) and anything they represent have "-s" or "-es" endings unlike other verbs.

| I   You (singular) |

🔸 "I" and "you"(singular) are singular subjects but require plural verbs. This is an exception to the subject-verb agreement rule.

| You (plural)   We   They |

🔸 These pronouns are plural subjects and, therefore, require plural verbs.

Now, let us examine the sentences below:

Persons	Sentences
First person singular (I)	I live in this house.
Second person singular (you)	You live in this house.
Third person singular (he)	He lives in this house.
Third person singular (she)	She lives in this house.
Third person singular (it)	It lives in this house.
First person plural (we)	We live in this house.
Second person plural (you)	You guys live in this house.
Third person plural (they)	They live in this house.

If you take a good look at these sentences, you will notice that "I" and "you"(singular) are singular subjects but are matched with the plural verb "live" as opposed to the subject-verb agreement rule. This is because they are exceptions to the rule that states that a singular subject takes a singular verb while a plural subject takes a plural verb. This rule applies only to the third-person singular subjects (he, she, and it), the first person plural subject (we), the second person plural subject (you), and the third person plural subject (they). Therefore, it would be wrong to say "I lives in this house" or "You lives in this house" simply because the subjects in question are singular.

4

CHAPTER 3

CONJUGATION OF VERBS

What is conjugation?

Conjugation is "the variation of the form of a verb, by which the voice, mood, tense, number, and person are identified" (*Concise Oxford English Dictionary*, 2011: 302).

Conjugation of verbs in grammar can be likened to the use of formulas in mathematics. Here are sixty examples of verbs in the active voice and present tense.

1

Be

Persons	Singular	Plural
First person	I am	We are
Second person	You are	You are
Third person	He is, She is, It is	They are

2

Do

Persons	Singular	Plural
First person	I do	We do
Second person	You do	You do
Third person	He does, She does, It does	They do

3

See

Persons	Singular	Plural
First person	I see	We see
Second person	You see	You see
Third person	He sees, She sees, It sees	They see

4
Know

Persons	Singular	Plural
First person	I know	We know
Second person	You know	You know
Third person	He knows, She knows, It knows	They know

5
Live

Persons	Singular	Plural
First person	I live	We live
Second person	You live	You live
Third person	He lives, She lives, It lives	They live

6
Love

Persons	Singular	Plural
First person	I love	We love
Second person	You love	You love
Third person	He loves, She loves, It loves	They love

7
Want

Persons	Singular	Plural
First person	I want	We want
Second person	You want	You want
Third person	He wants, She wants, It wants	They want

8
Teach

Persons	Singular	Plural
First person	I teach	We teach
Second person	You teach	You teach
Third person	He teaches, She teaches, It teaches	They teach

9
Make

Persons	Singular	Plural
First person	I make	We make
Second person	You make	You make
Third person	He makes, She makes, It makes	They make

10
Hear

Persons	Singular	Plural
First person	I hear	We hear
Second person	You hear	You hear
Third person	He hears, She hears, It hears	They hear

11
Keep

Persons	Singular	Plural
First person	I keep	We keep
Second person	You keep	You keep
Third person	He keeps, She keeps, It keeps	They keep

12
Write

Persons	Singular	Plural
First person	I write	We write
Second person	You write	You write
Third person	He writes, She writes, It writes	They write

13
Have

Persons	Singular	Plural
First person	I have	We have
Second person	You have	You have
Third person	He has, She has, It has	They have

14

Hold

Persons	Singular	Plural
First person	I hold	We hold
Second person	You hold	You hold
Third person	He holds, She holds, It holds	They hold

15

Go

Persons	Singular	Plural
First person	I go	We go
Second person	You go	You go
Third person	He goes, She goes, It goes	They go

16

Read

Persons	Singular	Plural
First person	I read	We read
Second person	You read	You read
Third person	He reads, She reads, It reads	They read

17

Spend

Persons	Singular	Plural
First person	I spend	We spend
Second person	You spend	You spend
Third person	He spends, She spends, It spends	They spend

18

Take

Persons	Singular	Plural
First person	I take	We take
Second person	You take	You take
Third person	He takes, She takes, It takes	They take

19
Pay

Persons	Singular	Plural
First person	I pay	We pay
Second person	You pay	You pay
Third person	He pays, She pays, It pays	They pay

20
Look

Persons	Singular	Plural
First person	I look	We look
Second person	You look	You look
Third person	He looks, She looks, It looks	They look

21
Possess

Persons	Singular	Plural
First person	I possess	We possess
Second person	You possess	You possess
Third person	He possesses, She possesses, It possesses	They possess

22
Understand

Persons	Singular	Plural
First person	I understand	We understand
Second person	You understand	You understand
Third person	He understands, She understands, It understands	They understand

23
Come

Persons	Singular	Plural
First person	I come	We come
Second person	You come	You come
Third person	He comes, She comes, It comes	They come

24

Like

Persons	Singular	Plural
First person	I like	We like
Second person	You like	You like
Third person	He likes, She likes, It likes	They like

25

Sleep

Persons	Singular	Plural
First person	I sleep	We sleep
Second person	You sleep	You sleep
Third person	He sleeps, She sleeps, It sleeps	They sleep

26

Say

Persons	Singular	Plural
First person	I say	We say
Second person	You say	You say
Third person	He says, She says, It says	They say

27

Speak

Persons	Singular	Plural
First person	I speak	We speak
Second person	You speak	You speak
Third person	He speaks, She speaks, It speaks	They speak

28

Travel

Persons	Singular	Plural
First person	I travel	We travel
Second person	You travel	You travel
Third person	He travels, She travels, It travels	They travel

29
Help

Persons	Singular	Plural
First person	I help	We help
Second person	You help	You help
Third person	He helps, She helps, It helps	They help

30
Belong

Persons	Singular	Plural
First person	I belong	We belong
Second person	You belong	You belong
Third person	He belongs, She belongs, It belongs	They belong

31
Celebrate

Persons	Singular	Plural
First person	I celebrate	We celebrate
Second person	You celebrate	You celebrate
Third person	He celebrates, She celebrates, It celebrates	They celebrate

32
Meet

Persons	Singular	Plural
First person	I meet	We meet
Second person	You meet	You meet
Third person	He meets, She meets, It meets	They meet

33
Arrive

Persons	Singular	Plural
First person	I arrive	We arrive
Second person	You arrive	You arrive
Third person	He arrives, She arrives, It arrives	They arrive

34
Carry

Persons	Singular	Plural
First person	I carry	We carry
Second person	You carry	You carry
Third person	He carries, She carries, It carries	They carry

35
Communicate

Persons	Singular	Plural
First person	I communicate	We communicate
Second person	You communicate	You communicate
Third person	He communicates, She communicates, It communicates	They communicate

36
Gesticulate

Persons	Singular	Plural
First person	I gesticulate	We gesticulate
Second person	You gesticulate	You gesticulate
Third person	He gesticulates, She gesticulates, It gesticulates	They gesticulate

37
Defend

Persons	Singular	Plural
First person	I defend	We defend
Second person	You defend	You defend
Third person	He defends, She defends, It defends	They defend

38
Need

Persons	Singular	Plural
First person	I need	We need
Second person	You need	You need
Third person	He needs, She needs, It needs	They need

39
Work

Persons	Singular	Plural
First person	I work	I work
Second person	You work	You work
Third person	He works, She works, It works	They work

40
Sell

Persons	Singular	Plural
First person	I sell	We sell
Second person	You sell	You sell
Third person	He sells, She sells, It sells	They sell

41
Sound

Persons	Singular	Plural
First person	I sound	We sound
Second person	You sound	You sound
Third person	He sounds, She sounds, It sounds	They sound

42
Sing

Persons	Singular	Plural
First person	I sing	We sing
Second person	You sing	You sing
Third person	He sings, She sings, It sings	They sing

43
Use

Persons	Singular	Plural
First person	I use	We use
Second person	You use	You use
Third person	He uses, She uses, It uses	They use

44
Yield

Persons	Singular	Plural
First person	I yield	We yield
Second person	You yield	You yield
Third person	He yields, She yields, It yields	They yield

45
Think

Persons	Singular	Plural
First person	I think	We think
Second person	You think	You think
Third person	He thinks, She thinks, It thinks	They think

46
Resemble

Persons	Singular	Plural
First person	I resemble	We resemble
Second person	You resemble	You resemble
Third person	He resembles, She resembles, It resembles	They resemble

47
Expect

Persons	Singular	Plural
First person	I expect	We expect
Second person	You expect	You expect
Third person	He expects, She expects, It expects	They expect

48
Kill

Persons	Singular	Plural
First person	I kill	We kill
Second person	You kill	You kill
Third person	He kills, She kills, It kills	They kill

49
Intend

Persons	Singular	Plural
First person	I intend	We intend
Second person	You intend	You intend
Third person	He intends, She intends, It intends	They intend

50
Jump

Persons	Singular	Plural
First person	I jump	We jump
Second person	You jump	You jump
Third person	He jumps, She jumps, It jumps	They jump

51
Seem

Persons	Singular	Plural
First person	I seem	We seem
Second person	You seem	You seem
Third person	He seems, She seems, It seems	They seem

52
Zip

Persons	Singular	Plural
First person	I zip	We zip
Second person	You zip	You zip
Third person	He zips, She zips, It zips	They zip

53
Grow

Persons	Singular	Plural
First person	I grow	We grow
Second person	You grow	You grow
Third person	He grows, She grows, It grows	They grow

54
Quarrel

Persons	Singular	Plural
First person	I quarrel	We quarrel
Second person	You quarrel	You quarrel
Third person	He quarrels, She quarrels, It quarrels	They quarrel

55
Adore

Persons	Singular	Plural
First person	I adore	We adore
Second person	You adore	You adore
Third person	He adores, She adores, It adores	They adore

56
Prefer

Persons	Singular	Plural
First person	I prefer	We prefer
Second person	You prefer	You prefer
Third person	He prefers, She prefers, It prefers	They prefer

57
Direct

Persons	Singular	Plural
First person	I direct	We direct
Second person	You direct	You direct
Third person	He directs, She directs, It directs	They direct

58
Enjoy

Persons	Singular	Plural
First person	I enjoy	We enjoy
Second person	You enjoy	You enjoy
Third person	He enjoys, She enjoys, It enjoys	They enjoy

59
Feel

Persons	Singular	Plural
First person	I feel	We feel
Second person	You feel	You feel
Third person	He feels, She feels, It feels	They feel

60
Begin

Persons	Singular	Plural
First person	I begin	We begin
Second person	You begin	You begin
Third person	He begins, She begins, It begins	They begin

CHAPTER 4

DEFECTIVE SENTENCES AND THEIR CORRECT FORMS (1)

What is *defective*?

Defective means "faulty" (*Merriam-Webster's Dictionary of Basic English*, 2009: 176).

In view of the above definition, defective sentences can therefore be defined as faulty words expressing a statement, a question, or an order. To put it simply: Defective sentences = incorrect sentences.

In the sentences below, it is necessary to note the following:

* ❖ All the verbs cited here are drawn from chapter 3.
* ❖ PS = plural subject
* ❖ PV = plural verb
* ❖ SS = singular subject
* ❖ SV = singular verb

1a. People does not like teaching. (Incorrect)

 b. People do not like teaching. (Correct)

   PS   PV

 Justification: People = they (see example 2)

2a. The students knows the answer. (Incorrect)

 b. The students know the answer. (Correct)

   ↑   ↑
   PS   PV

 Justification: students = they (see example 4)

3a. The young girl look so charming. (Incorrect)

b. The young girl looks so charming. (Correct)

   SS SV

   Justification: young girl = she (see example 20)

4a. It pay to be honest. (Incorrect)

b. It pays to be honest. (Correct)

SS SV

   Justification: It (see example 19)

5a. God love a cheerful giver. (Incorrect)

b. God loves a cheerful giver. (Correct)

SS   SV

   Justification: God = he (see example 6)

6a. Those pupils writes very well. (Incorrect)

b. Those pupils write very well. (Correct)

   ↑   ↑
   PS   PV

   Justification: pupils = they (see example 12)

7a. Jesus love little children. (Incorrect)

b. Jesus loves little children. (Correct)

   ↑   ↑
   SS   SV

   Justification: Jesus = he (see example 6)

8a. The cars belongs to my friend. (Incorrect)

b. The cars belong to my friend. (Correct)

PS   PV

Justification: cars = they (see example 30)

9a. Government workers is threatening to go on strike. (Incorrect)

b. Government workers are threatening to go on strike. (Correct)

PS   PV

Justification: workers = they (see example 1)

10a. The permanent secretary of this ministry do not take bribes. (Incorrect)

b. The permanent secretary of this ministry does not take bribes. (Correct)

SS   SV

Justification: permanent secretary = he or she (see example 2)

11a. Amaka and Chidi prefers singing to dancing. (Incorrect)

b. Amaka and Chidi prefer singing to dancing. (Correct)

PS   PV

Justification: Amaka + Chidi = they (see example 56)

12a. The Nigerian president live in Aso Rock. (Incorrect)

b. The Nigerian president lives in Aso Rock. (Correct)

SS   SV

Justification: The Nigerian president = he (see example 5)

13a.   My neighbours travels very often. (Incorrect)

 b.   My neighbours travel very often. (Correct)

PS   PV

Justification: neighbours = they (see example 28)

14a.   The girl have a pink bag. (Incorrect)

 b.   The girl has a pink bag. (Correct)

SS   SV

Justification: girl = she (see example 13)

15a.   Samuel have a very good memory. (Incorrect)

 b.   Samuel has a very good memory. (Correct)

SS   SV

Justification: Samuel = he (see example 13)

16a.   The lecturer speak excellent English. (Incorrect)

 b.   The lecturer speaks excellent English. (Correct)

SS   SV

Justification: lecturer = he or she (see example 27)

17a.   The drug help to take away pain. (Incorrect)

 b.   The drug helps to take away pain. (Correct)

SS   SV

Justification: drug = it (see example 29)

18a. Christians celebrates Christmas. (Incorrect)

b. Christians celebrate Christmas. (Correct)

   PS   PV

   Justification: Christians = they (see example 31)

19a. My colleague and I has passed the Civil Service compulsory examination. (Incorrect)

b. My colleague and I have passed the Civil Service compulsory examination. (Correct)

   PS   PV

   Justification: My colleague + I = we (see example 13)

20a. The boys does not realise how much they bore us. (Incorrect)

b. The boys do not realise how much they bore us. (Correct)

   PS   PV

   Justification: boys = they (see example 2)

21a. God's people is praying and fasting. (Incorrect)

b. God's people are praying and fasting. (Correct)

   PS   PV

   Justification: God's people = they (see example 1)

22a. The students enjoys reading novels. (Incorrect)

b. The students enjoy reading novels. (Correct)

   PS   PV

   Justification: students = they (see example 58)

23a. This knife look blunt. (Incorrect)

b. This knife looks blunt. (Correct)

SS   SV

Justification: knife = it (see example 20)

24a. Evelyn and Edith directs a large choir. (Incorrect)

b. Evelyn and Edith direct a large choir. (Correct)

PS   PV

Justification: Evelyn + Edith = they (see example 57)

25a. Iroko trees grows very tall. (Incorrect)

b. Iroko trees grow very tall. (Correct)

PS   PV

Justification: Iroko trees = they (see example 53)

26a. The cutlass belong to my uncle. (Incorrect)

b. The cutlass belongs to my uncle. (Correct)

SS   SV

Justification: cutlass = it (see example 30)

27a. The price of beans are going up tomorrow. (Incorrect)

b. The price of beans is going up tomorrow. (Correct)

SS   SV

Justification: price = it (see example 1)

28a.   Let's run through the agenda before the manager and his assistant arrives. (Incorrect)

b.   Let's run through the agenda before the manager and his assistant arrive. (Correct)

PS   PV

Justification: the manager + his assistant = they (see example 33)

29a.   Babatunde adore his fiancée. (Incorrect)

b.   Babatunde adores his fiancée. (Correct)

SS   SV

Justification: Babatunde = he (see example 55)

30a.   My children is very brilliant. (Incorrect)

b.   My children are very brilliant. (Correct)

PS   PV

Justification: children = they (see example 1)

31a.   The farm belong to my stepfather. (Incorrect)

b.   The farm belongs to my stepfather. (Correct)

SS   SV

Justification: farm = it (see example 30)

32a.   The offence carry a fine of $500. (Incorrect)

b.   The offence carries a fine of $500. (Correct)

SS   SV

Justification: offence = it (see example 34)

24

33a. The poem communicate the poet's despair. (Incorrect)

b. The poem communicates the poet's despair. (Correct)

Justification: poem = it (see example 35)

34a. Pearl gesticulate often. (Incorrect)

b. Pearl gesticulates often. (Correct)

Justification: Pearl = she (see example 36)

35a. Barrister Eunice always defend her daughter. (Incorrect)

b. Barrister Eunice always defends her daughter. (Correct)

Justification: Barrister Eunice = she (see example 37)

36a. The children feels like a cup of tea. (Incorrect)

b. The children feel like a cup of tea. (Correct)

Justification: children = they (see example 59)

37a. My husband and I has decided to retire. (Incorrect)

b. My husband and I have decided to retire. (Correct)

Justification: My husband + I = we (see example 13)

38a. Tina's fiancé have a complete disregard for her feelings. (Incorrect)

b. Tina's fiancé has a complete disregard for her feelings. (Correct)

    ↑   ↑
   SS SV

Justification: Tina's fiancé = he (see example 13)

39a. Afam intend to study accountancy. (Incorrect)

b. Afam intends to study accountancy. (Correct)

   ↑ ↑
  SS SV

Justification: Afam = he (see example 49)

40a. Henry often jump to conclusions. (Incorrect)

b. Henry often jumps to conclusions. (Correct)

  ↑   ↑
  SS   SV

Justification: Henry = he (see example 50)

41a. Victor are a man of his words. (Incorrect)

b. Victor is a man of his words. (Correct)

  ↑ ↑
  SS SV

Justification: Victor = he (see example 1)

42a. The old woman live in a hut. (Incorrect)

b. The old woman lives in a hut. (Correct)

   ↑   ↑
  SS SV

Justification: old woman = she (see example 5)

43a. Incessant noise from the street make our work difficult. (Incorrect)

b. Incessant noise from the street makes our work difficult. (Correct)

      ↑   ↑

     SS   SV

Justification: Incessant noise = it (see example 9)

44a. Agatha need to go to a driving school. (Incorrect)

b. Agatha needs to go to a driving school. (Correct)

  ↑ ↑

 SS SV

Justification: Agatha = she (see example 38)

45a. Festus always quarrel at the slightest provocation. (Incorrect)

b. Festus always quarrels at the slightest provocation. (Correct)

  ↑   ↑

 SS   SV

Justification: Festus = he (see example 54)

46a. Nkechi work in the Ministry of Higher Education. (Incorrect)

b. Nkechi works in the Ministry of Higher Education. (Correct)

  ↑ ↑

 SS SV

Justification: Nkechi = she (see example 39)

47a. These traders sells crayfish at the Ogbe-Ogonogo modern market. (Incorrect)

b. These traders sell crayfish at the Ogbe-Ogonogo modern market. (Correct)

  ↑ ↑

 PS PV

Justification: traders = they (see example 40)

48a.   Your new job sound too jammy to be true. (Incorrect)

b.   Your new job sounds too jammy to be true. (Correct)
      ↑   ↑
     SS   SV

Justification: new job = it (see example 41)

49a.   Kelvin speak in an effeminate manner. (Incorrect)

b.   Kelvin speaks in an effeminate manner. (Correct)
     ↑   ↑
   SS   SV

Justification: Kelvin = he (see example 27)

50a.   The nurses seems to be in a hurry. (Incorrect)

b.   The nurses seem to be in a hurry. (Correct)
     ↑   ↑
   PS PV

Justification: nurses = they (see example 51)

51a.   Ejiro and I sings in the church choir. (Incorrect)

b.   Ejiro and I sing in the church choir. (Correct)
    ↖↗ ↑
   PS PV

Justification: Ejiro + I = we (see example 42)

52a.   It take character to do a thing like that. (Incorrect)

b.   It takes character to do a thing like that. (Correct)
   ↑ ↑
  SS SV

Justification: It (see example 18)

28

53a. Angela use her maiden name for professional purposes. (Incorrect)

b. Angela uses her maiden name for professional purposes. (Correct)

↑ ↑
SS SV

Justification: Angela = she (see example 43)

54a. Bridget want to do her assignment. (Incorrect)

b. Bridget wants to do her assignment. (Correct)

↑ ↑
SS SV

Justification: Bridget = she (see example 7)

55a. Bose rarely yield to pressure. (Incorrect)

b. Bose rarely yields to pressure. (Correct)

↑ ↑
SS SV

Justification: Bose = she (see example 44)

56a. Vera's blouse zip up at the back. (Incorrect)

b. Vera's blouse zips up at the back. (Correct)

↑ ↑
SS SV

Justification: blouse = it (see example 52)

57a. Uche want the best of everything. (Incorrect)

b. Uche wants the best of everything. (Correct)

↑ ↑
SS SV

Justification: Uche = he or she (see example 7)

58a. Olu use his car for commercial purposes. (Incorrect)

  b. Olu uses his car for commercial purposes. (Correct)
      ↑   ↑
      SS SV

      Justification: Olu = he (see example 43)

59a. List five items that begins with the letter A. (Incorrect)

  b. List five items that begin with the letter A. (Correct)
         ↑   ↑
         PS   PV

      Justification: items = they (see example 60)

60a. Hairdressers in this town meets on Tuesdays. (Incorrect)

  b. Hairdressers in this town meet on Tuesdays. (Correct)
         ↑   ↑
         PS   PV

      Justification: Hairdressers = they (see example 32)

CHAPTER 5

DEFECTIVE SENTENCES AND THEIR CORRECT FORMS (2)

No matter the profession, the importance of speaking good English cannot be overemphasized. This is because the ability to speak correctly gives a person in business or in social circles a lot of advantages. Here are some examples:

Teacher

Just imagine a teacher writing these sentences on the board for students to copy.

Incorrect sentences

No.	Words	Sentences
1.	Days	Seven days makes one week.
2.	Words	List five words that begins with the letter **K**.
3.	Object	Draw an object that start with the letter O.
4.	Weeks	Four weeks makes one month.
5.	Baby	My baby like drinking milk.
6.	Teachers	Good teachers inspires their students.
7.	Sixty	Sixty seconds makes a minute.

Question: Do you think this teacher can impart the right knowledge?

Correct sentences

No.	Words	Sentences
1.	Days	Seven days make one week. ↑ ↑ PS PV
2.	Words	List five words that begin with the letter K. ↑ ↑ PS PV
3.	Object	Draw an object that starts with the letter O. ↑ ↑ SS SV

4.	Weeks	Four weeks make one month. ↑ ↑ PS PV
5.	Baby	My baby likes drinking milk. ↑ ↑ SS SV
6.	Teachers	Good teachers inspire their students. ↑ ↑ PS PV
7.	Seconds	Sixty seconds make a minute. ↑ ↑ PS PV

A lawyer in the courtroom

Incorrect sentences

Lawyer: Has you lived in this house all your life?
Witness: Yes.
Lawyer: Does you live with your parents?
Witness: Yes.
Lawyer: Is your parents aware of this incident?

Obviously, this kind of lawyer who lacks a good command of English cannot confidently represent his clients in a court of law.

Correct sentences (lawyer)

1. Have you lived in this house all your life?

    PV SS

2. Do you live with your parents?

    PV SS

3. Are your parents aware of this incident?

    PV   PS

Pharmacist

Incorrect sentences

1. This drug are to be taken three times daily.
2. If the patient remain with a fever in three days or the symptoms does not improve, consult a physician.

Note: A pharmacist who lacks the right grammatical expressions is likely to be misunderstood.

Correct sentences

1. This drug is to be taken three times daily.

    SS SV

2. If the patient remains with a fever in three days or symptoms do not improve, consult a doctor.

    SS   SV   PS   PV

Applicant

Incorrect sentences

1. I understands there is a vacancy in your company.
2. I possesses a master's degree in philosophy.
3. I hopes to do my best if I am employed.

Note: No right-thinking employer will employ a graduate who speaks like this.

Correct sentences

1. I understand there is a vacancy in your company.

    SS PV

2. I possess a master's degree in philosophy.

    SS PV

33

3.   I hope to do my best if I am employed.

SS PV

Justification:

The sentences above appear to be wrong because the singular subjects are matched with plural verbs. If you flash your mind back to chapter 2, you will remember that there is an exception to the subject-verb agreement rule. This has to do with the first- and second-person pronouns "I" and "you," which are singular subjects but require plural verbs (singular subjects + plural verbs). From all indications, it is clear that the applicant is not aware of this fact.

Conversation of a young man with a young girl

Incorrect sentences

Young man:	Hello, baby, how is you?
Young girl:	(Thinking he made a mistake) I'm good.
Young man:	My name are Jimmy Okafor.
Young girl:	I'm Uche.
Young man:	I loves you and want you to be my girlfriend.
Young girl:	(Obviously disgusted) I'm not interested.
Young man:	Come on, baby, where does you live?
Young girl:	(Totally disgusted) I beg to take my leave. (Walks away)

Note: If you take a look at the sentences above, you will observe that the young man's English is totally defective and cannot impress any intelligent young girl.

Correct sentences (the young man)

1.   Hello, baby, how are you?

PV SS

2.   My name is Jimmy Okafor.

SS SV

3. I love you and want you to be my girlfriend.

    SS PV

4. Where do you live?

    PV SS

Office boy

Incorrect sentences

1. I understands your language.
2. My boss are not in the office.
3. The director and the manager of this company is in a meeting.
4. The secretary do not type quickly.

Note: This kind of office boy will certainly give a bad impression of the company that hired him.

Correct sentences

1. I understand your language.

    SS   PV

2. My boss is not in the office.

    SS SV

3. The director and the manager of this company are in a meeting.

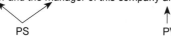

         PS   PV

4. The secretary does not type quickly.

    SS   SV

Sales boy

Incorrect sentences

1. Our customers is very reliable.
2. People likes patronizing us.
3. We produces durable goods.

Note: No sales manager will employ a sales boy who speaks in this manner.

Correct sentences

1. Our customers are very reliable.

    PS   PV

2. People like patronizing us.

    PS   PV

3. We produce durable goods.

    PS   PV

CHAPTER 6

ADDITIONAL FACTS ON SUBJECT-VERB AGREEMENT

Despite the fact that this rule looks simple, a lot of difficulties are encountered in trying to make the subject agree with the verb. Here are some examples:

1

Linking of compound subject with "and"

When two or more subjects are connected with "and," the subject is plural and, therefore, requires a plural verb.

Examples:

1. A car and a house are my immediate needs.
    ↑   ↑   ↑
    SS1   SS2   PV

    Justification: car + house = plural subject

    are = plural verb

2. Tola, Funke, and Seyi are going home.
    ↑   ↑   ↑   ↑
    SS1   SS2   SS3 PV

    Justification: Tola + Funke + Seyi = plural subject

    are = plural verb

3. Irene, Harmony, and Uche are my sisters.
    ↑   ↑   ↑   ↑
    SS1   SS2   SS3 PV

Justification: Irene + Harmony + Uche = plural subject

are = plural verb

4. Gloria and her husband love their children.

SS1   SS2   PV

Justification: Gloria + her husband = plural subject

love = plural verb

5. Usain Bolt, Yohan Blake, and Warren Weir are Jamaicans.

SS1   SS2   SS3 PV

Justification: Usain Bolt + Yohan Blake + Warren Weir = plural subject

are = plural verb

6. Canada, the United States, and Mexico are North American countries.

SS1   SS2   SS3 PV

Justification: Canada + the United States + Mexico = plural subject

are = plural verb

Note:
There is an exception to this rule. When two subjects connected with "and" refer to the same person or thing, the subject is singular and, therefore, requires a singular verb.

Examples:

1. The director and administrator is addressing the staff. (same person)

Justification: The director + administrator = singular subject

is = singular verb

2.   The president and chairman is very tactful. (same person)

Justification: The president + chairman = singular subject

is = singular verb

But if the subjects in the above sentences refer to two individuals, the verbs should be plural.

Examples:

1.   The director and the administrator are addressing the staff. (two individuals)

Justification: The director + the administrator = plural subject

are = plural verb

2.   The president and the chairman are very tactful. (two individuals)

Justification: The president + the chairman = plural subject

are = plural verb

Note: By placing the definite article "the" before administrator and chairman, it is obvious that two people are involved.

2
Linking of two singular subjects with "or" or "nor,"
"either or" or "neither nor"

When two singular subjects are connected with "or" or "nor," the verb is singular. Also, when two singular subjects are connected with "either or" or "neither nor," the same rule applies.

Examples:

1a.   My daddy or mummy is travelling today. (Correct)

b.   My daddy or mummy are travelling today. (Incorrect)

Justification: My daddy or mummy = singular subject

is = singular verb

2a.   The hairdresser or her apprentice is in the salon. (Correct)

b.   The hairdresser or her apprentice are in the salon. (Incorrect)

Justification: The hairdresser or her apprentice = singular subject

is = singular verb

3a.   Either Pastor E.A. Adeboye or Pastor Sam Onitiri is preaching. (Correct)

b.   Either Pastor E.A. Adeboye or Pastor Sam Onitiri are preaching. (Incorrect)

Justification: Pastor E.A. Adeboye or Pastor Sam Onitiri = singular subject

is = singular verb

4a.   Neither the doctor nor the nurse is willing to help the penniless patient. (Correct)

b.   Neither the doctor nor the nurse are willing to help the penniless patient. (Incorrect)

Justification: The doctor nor the nurse = singular subject

is = singular verb

5a.   Neither the seller nor the buyer is prepared to come to an agreement. (Correct)

b.   Neither the seller nor the buyer are prepared to come to an agreement. (Incorrect)

Justification: The seller nor the buyer = singular subject

is = singular verb

6a.   Neither the lecturer nor the student is ready to leave. (Correct)

b.   Neither the lecturer nor the student are ready to leave. (Incorrect)

Justification: The lecturer nor the student = singular subject

is = singular verb

7a. Either the chairman or his deputy is presiding at the meeting. (Correct)

  b. Either the chairman or his deputy are presiding at the meeting. (Incorrect)

Justification: The chairman or his deputy = singular subject

is = singular verb

8a. Either the commissioner or the permanent secretary is responsibility for the delay. (Correct)

  b. Either the commissioner or the permanent secretary are responsibility for the delay. (Incorrect)

Justification: The commissioner or the permanent secretary = singular subject

is = singular verb

3

Closer subject

When one of the subjects connected with the indefinite pronouns "either or" or "neither nor" is singular and the other plural, the verb agrees with the subject that is closer to it. When both subjects are plural, the verb is also plural.

Examples:

1. Neither the prostitutes in this room nor the one next door is willing to change.

Justification: The one next door = closer subject (singular)

is = singular verb

2. Either the newspaper vendor or his customers are littering the floor with old newspapers.

Justification: His customers = closer subject (plural)

are = plural verb

3. Neither the footballers nor their fans are happy.

Justification: The footballers + their fans = plural subject

are = plural verb

Note:

In the first sentence, the singular subject is closer to the verb. In the second sentence, the plural subject is closer to the verb. Finally, in the third sentence, both subjects are plural, hence the plural verb "are." In the above examples, agreement depends on the placement of the subject.

4
Nouns that are plural in form but singular in meaning

Some nouns appear to be plural but are actually singular in meaning and require singular verbs.

1. News:

Bad news travels very fast.
SS   SV

2. Measles:

Measles is an infectious disease.
SS   SV

3. Civics:

Civics is an interesting subject.
SS SV

4. Mumps:

    Mumps is a disease that causes painful swelling in the neck.

    SS   SV

5. Physics:

    Physics is not a core subject.

    SS   SV

5
Nouns that are plural in form and meaning

Some nouns are plural in form and meaning. These nouns require plural verbs.

Examples:

1. Scissors:

    The scissors have caused severe damage.

    PS   PV

2. Goods:

    These goods are durable.

    PS   PV

3. Thanks:

    Thanks are due to all those who made meaningful contributions to charity.

    PS   PV

4.   Shears:

My father's shears are very blunt.

PS   PV

5.   Tongs:

Tongs are used for picking up and holding things.

PS   PV

6.   Tweezers:

These tweezers are used for pulling out my mother's grey hair.

PS   PV

7.   Pants:

My baby's pants are clean.

PS   PV

8.   Pliers:

The pliers are for the technician.

PS   PV

9.   Glasses:

My glasses are tinted.

PS   PV

10. Trousers:

His trousers are very dirty.

PS   PV

Note:
Some of these plural nouns can be matched with singular verbs if they are preceded by the word "pair," which becomes the subject of the sentence.

Examples:

1. A pair of scissors is on the table.

Here, "pair" is the subject, hence the singular verb "is."

2. My pair of glasses is very expensive.
3. Ada's pair of pants is extra large.
4. Kunle's new pair of trousers is very tight.

6
Another group of nouns are plural in form
but singular or plural in meaning

These nouns end in "-ics." When they are singular, they require singular verbs. When they are plural, they require plural verbs.

Examples:

-ics nouns	Singular	Plural
Statistics	Statistics is a subject that is easy to understand.	Statistics show that the birth rate is high.
Economics	Economics is the study of how a society organizes its money, trade, and industry.	The economics of the project are very encouraging.
Politics	Politics is a dirty game.	Okonkwo's politics are moderate.

7
Indefinite pronouns

These are pronouns that do not refer to any person or thing in particular. Some are singular and, therefore, require singular verbs.

Examples:

1. Either:

    Either of the twins has gone to the market.

    SS   SV

2. Neither:

    Neither of them is reasonable.

    SS   SV

3. Each:

    Each of the women is cooking fried rice.

    SS   SV

4. One:

    One of my friends is celebrating her birthday today.

    SS   SV

5. No one:

    No one is in the room.

    ↑ ↑

    SS SV

6. Nobody:

    Nobody is willing to stay.

    SS SV

7. Somebody:

   Somebody is against the decision.

   SS   SV

8. Everybody:

   Everybody knows you.

   SS   SV

9. Anyone:

   Anyone has the right to say no.

   SS   SV

10. Anybody:

    Anybody is free to negotiate.

    SS   SV

8

Some indefinite pronouns are plural and,
therefore, require plural verbs.

Examples:

1. Several:

   Several of the official files have been destroyed by fire.

   PS   PV

2. Few:

    A few of the students were punished.

    PS   PV

3. Both:

    Both are to travel abroad.

    PS PV

4. Many:

    Many of the graduates are from Nigeria.

    PS   PV

9

Some indefinite pronouns are either singular or plural.

Furthermore, just like the collective nouns, some indefinite pronouns are either singular or plural, depending on what they refer to in a sentence. For instance, if they refer to an uncountable noun, a singular verb is used. But if they refer to a countable noun, it is important to find out whether the noun is singular or plural. If it is singular, use a singular verb, but if it is plural, use a plural verb.

Examples:

Indefinite pronouns	Singular	Plural
Some	Some of the juice contains no artificial preservatives. Some refers to "juice." Juice is uncountable. Therefore, it is singular, hence the singular verb "contains."	Some of the ceramic tiles are very expensive. Some refers to "ceramic tiles." Therefore, it is plural, hence the plural verb "are."
All	All of the salt is in the plastic bottle. All refers to "salt." Salt is uncountable. Therefore, it is singular, hence the singular verb "is."	All of the knives are sharp. All refers to "knives." Therefore, it is plural, hence the plural verb "are."

Any	Is any afflicted? Let him pray. Any refers to "him." Therefore, it is singular, hence the singular verb "is."	Are any of the applicants from Ghana coming for the interview? Any refers to "applicants." Therefore, it is plural, hence the plural verb "are."
Most	Most of the water has spilled onto the floor. Most refers to "water." Water is uncountable. Therefore, it is singular, hence the singular verb "has."	Most of the drugs are not harmful. Most refers to "drugs." Therefore, it is plural, hence the plural verb "are."
None	None of the pap is left for the baby. None refers to "pap." Pap is uncountable. Therefore, it is singular, hence the singular verb "is."	None of these bags are expensive. None refers to "bags." Therefore, it is plural, hence the plural verb "are."

10

Positive subject

Sometimes a sentence is composed of a positive and a negative subject, whereby one is plural and the other is singular. In this case, the verb should agree with the positive subject.

Examples:

1. It is not the children but their mother who is cooking.

    Justification: mother = positive subject (singular)

    is = singular verb

2. It was the commissioner, not his ideas, who has provoked the administrative officers.

    Justification: commissioner = positive subject (singular)

    has = singular verb

3. It was the trader, not her goods, who has attracted the customers.

    Justification: trader = positive subject (singular)

    has = singular verb

11

Prepositional phrase

Prepositional phrase simply means a preposition and the noun next to it, which serves as the object of the preposition. Simply put, a prepositional phrase = a preposition + succeeding noun. Occasionally, the subject is separated from the verb by prepositional phrases, such as "as well as," "together with," "along with," "in addition to," and "including." These expressions should be overlooked when considering whether to use a singular or plural verb. This is because they are not the same as "and" and can never contain the subject.

Examples:

1.   Tolu, as well as Funmi, speaks English.

Note:
The skeleton of this sentence is "Tolu speaks English." The prepositional phrase "as well as Funmi" does not affect the subject of the sentence, but only modifies it.

2.   The lecturer, <u>together with his students,</u> is in the room.

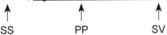

    SS   PP   SV

3.   These new laws, <u>together with the old one,</u> show that the company is organized.

    PS   PP   PV

4.   Poverty, <u>as well as pride,</u> is the reason for his pitiable condition.

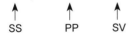

    SS   PP   SV

5.   The car key, <u>as well as the envelopes,</u> is in the handbag.

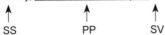

    SS   PP   SV

6.   John, <u>including his brothers,</u> is doing very well at school.

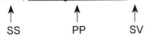

    SS   PP   SV

7. Agnes, <u>together with her sisters,</u> plans to visit Paris next year.

   SS   PP   SV

8. Milk, <u>in addition to crayfish,</u> is a good source of protein.

   SS   PP   SV

9. The surgeon, <u>along with two nurses,</u> is in the theatre.

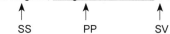

   SS   PP   SV

10. Yam, <u>in addition to rice,</u> is a source of carbohydrate.

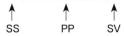

   SS   PP   SV

11. The dog, <u>together with its puppies,</u> is in the cage.

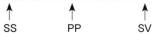

   SS   PP   SV

12. Garlic, <u>in addition to ginger,</u> is a medicinal spice.

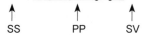

   SS   PP   SV

13. The taxi driver, <u>including his passengers,</u> is in the car.

   SS   PP   SV

12
Collective noun

A collective noun is a singular noun that refers to a group of people, animals, or things. It is either singular or plural depending on how it is used in the sentence. For instance, if members of a group are acting as a unit, it is singular and, therefore, requires a singular verb. But if they are acting separately, it is plural and, therefore, requires a plural verb.

Examples:

Collective nouns	Singular	Plural
Staff	The staff is having a meeting in the hall. Justification: staff = singular subject is = singular verb	The staff have secured loans for the purchase of their own personal vehicles. Justification: staff = plural subject have = plural verb
Committee	The committee is made up of three women and five men. Justification: committee = singular subject is = singular verb	The committee are having breakfast. Justification: committee = plural subject are = plural verb
Union	The union is meeting tomorrow morning. Justification: union = singular subject is = singular verb	The union are invited to give their opinions on the issue. Justification: union = plural subject are = plural verb
Family	The family consists of father, mother, and children. Justification: family = singular subject consists = singular verb	The family are unpacking their bags after a long journey. Justification: family = plural subject are = plural verb
Couple	The couple is celebrating Christmas in Nigeria. Justification: couple = singular subject is = singular verb	The couple are brushing their teeth. Justification: couple = plural subject are = plural verb
Orchestra	The orchestra is playing my children's favourite music. Justification: orchestra = singular subject is = singular verb	The orchestra are returning to their homes after a wonderful performance. Justification: orchestra = plural subject are = plural verb
Audience	The audience is watching a very interesting movie. Justification: audience = singular subject is = singular verb	The audience are waving their hands. Justification: audience = plural subject are = plural verb
Team	The team is performing excellently. Justification: team = singular subject is = singular verb	The team are receiving their gold, silver, and bronze medals. Justification: team = plural subject are = plural verb

Jury	The jury decides the facts in the case. Justification: jury = singular subject decides = singular verb	The jury are seated in the boxed-in area on one side of the courtroom. Justification: jury = plural subject are = plural verb
Class	The class is listening to a lecture on African literature. Justification: class = singular subject is = singular verb	The class are submitting their examination papers. Justification: class = plural subject are = plural verb
Herd	A herd of cows is moving northward. Justification: herd = singular subject is = singular verb	A herd of cows are grazing. Justification: herd = plural subject are = plural verb
Public	The public has a right to know what is contained in the budget. Justification: public = singular subject has = singular verb	The public have sent a number of complaints about kidnapping by terrorists. Justification: public = plural subject have = plural verb
Club	The club is admitting twenty new members. Justification: club = singular subject is = singular verb	The club are casting their votes. Justification: club = plural subject are = plural verb

Note:

When the members of a group are acting separately, use expressions such as "the members of the committee," "the members of staff," "the members of the family," among others. This makes the individuality more obvious.

13
Plural nouns

When a plural noun shows quantity, extent, weight, and period, it is considered singular and, therefore, requires a singular verb.

Examples:

1. <u>Forty-five inches</u> is the exact measurement. (Extent)

    SS   SV

2.   <u>Two kilos</u> is the weight of that white chicken. (Weight)

    SS   SV

3.   <u>Sixty thousand naira</u> is required for the purchase of office stationery. (Quantity)

    SS   SV

4.   <u>Five miles</u> is a long distance to walk. (Extent)

    SS   SV

5.   <u>Ten thousand naira</u> is all I need for the trip. (Quantity)

    SS   SV

6.   <u>Thirty miles</u> is a long way to jog. (Extent)

    SS   SV

7.   <u>Thirty-five months</u> is a long time to be pregnant. (Period)
    SS   SV

14
Half and part

The words "half" and "part" are singular or plural depending on what they refer to in a sentence. When they refer to a section, they are singular and require singular verbs. When they refer to a number of individuals or things, they are plural and, therefore, require plural verbs.

Examples:

1.   Half of Stella's birthday cake is left. (Section = singular)

    SS SV

2. Half of the workers are in the office. (Number = plural)

     PS   PV

3. Part of the building is undergoing renovation. (Section = singular)

     SS   SV

4. Part of the teachers have resigned. (Number = plural)

     PS   PV

5. Part of the factory workers are graduates. (Number = plural)

     PS   PV

6. Half a loaf is better than no bread. (Section = singular)

   SS SV

7. Half of the work is already finished. (Section = singular)

   SS SV

15
Title of a book or name of a firm

When the title of a book or the name of a firm is used as the subject of a sentence, use a singular verb.

Examples:

1. *Sons and Lovers* is a book by D.H. Lawrence.

    Justification: *Sons and Lovers* = singular subject

    is = singular verb

2. *The Beautyful Ones Are Not Yet Born* is a book that examines the spiritual and moral decay of the immediate post-independence Ghanaian society.

    Justification: *The Beautyful Ones Are Not Yet Born* = singular subject

    is = singular verb

3. Mr. Biggs is a fast food restaurant.

    Justification: Mr. Biggs = singular subject

    is = singular verb

4. Zinos, a fast food restaurant, is a good relaxation spot.

    Justification: Zinos = singular subject

    is = singular verb

5. James Gardens is known for its flower gardens, store pathway, and mature trees.

    Justification: James Gardens = singular subject

    is = singular verb

6. Mosaic Foods offers catering services.

    Justification: Mosaic Foods = singular subject

    Offers = singular verb

Note:
Ignore the plural form of the subject.

16

Contractions

A contraction is the short form of two words. When writing contractions, it is important to note that:

1. The two words are written as one word.
2. An apostrophe is used to show that one or more letters have been left out.

As usual, match a singular verb with a singular subject and a plural verb with a plural subject.

Examples:

Singular	Meaning	Plural	Meaning
Doesn't	Does not	Don't	Do not
Hasn't	Has not	Haven't	Have not
Isn't	Is not	Aren't	Are not

1a. Your mother don't like dogs. (Incorrect)

b. Your mother doesn't like dogs. (Correct)

Justification: Your mother = she (singular subject)

doesn't = singular verb

2a. Paul and Peter isn't happy. (Incorrect)

b. Paul and Peter aren't happy. (Correct)

Justification: Paul + Peter = they (plural subject)

aren't = plural verb

3a. The new immigrant haven't passed the driving test. (Incorrect)

b. The new immigrant hasn't passed the driving test. (Correct)

Justification: The new immigrant = he or she (singular subject)

hasn't = singular verb

17

Sentences that begin with "here" or "there"

When sentences begin with "here" or "there," the verb always comes before the subject, and they must agree.

Here

Examples:

Singular	Plural
Here is the pencil. SV SS	Here are the pencils. PV PS
Here is the book. SV SS	Here are the books. PV PS
Here is the apple. SV SS	Here are the apples. PV PS
Here is the washroom. SV SS	Here are the washrooms. PV PS

There

Examples:

Singular	Plural
There is a student in the classroom. SV SS	There are six students in the classroom. PV PS
There is a pot on the gas cooker. SV SS	There are three pots on the gas cooker. PV PS
There is a dirty plate in the sink. SV SS	There are dirty plates in the sink. PV PS
There is a school around the corner. SV SS	There are schools around the corner. PV PS

QUESTIONS

Copy the following sentences by supplying the verb that agrees with the subject.

1.   Women — been relegated to the background. (have, has)
2.   Lizzy's parents — like her choice of friends. (do not, does not)
3.   Mrs. Ajayi's children — all very insolent. (is, are)
4.   Victory — inevitable. (look, looks)
5.   I — it's going to rain. (think, thinks)
6.   Mama Iyabor — potatoes in Onitsha main market. (sells, sell)
7.   Emeka — three languages. (speaks, speak)
8.   I — beans to rice. (prefers, prefer)
9.   Felix — a junior position in the company. (occupies, occupy)
10. Ngozi — reading novels. (enjoy, enjoys)
11. Usain Bolt — the fastest man in the world. (is, are)
12. My family and I — relocating to Canada. (is, are)

Exercise B

Make sentences with the verbs below. Ensure that the verbs agree with the subjects.

1.   sings
2.   makes
3.   obey
4.   listen
5.   swim
6.   run
7.   stand
8.   seek
9.   love
10. cares
11. appreciate
12. give

Exercise C

Rewrite the sentences below by inserting the appropriate verb.

1. God <u>are</u> not a man that He should lie.
2. What <u>does</u> you want?
3. I can't <u>says</u> I blame Ade for resigning.
4. You <u>lacks</u> good manners.
5. Emmanuella <u>have</u> just received her appointment letter.
6. Samuel and Ehioma <u>writes</u> very well.
7. I <u>admires</u> your stance on education.
8. Uche <u>charm</u> everyone she meets.

Exercise D

Complete the following sentences using the correct one of the two verbs in brackets.

1. Amadi (like, likes) playing the clown.
2. Jesse (is, are) a very happy child.
3. All his life, he (have, has) been insulated from the harsh realities of the world.
4. God (is, are) not a respecter of persons.
5. These musical instruments (are, is) very expensive.
6. Chief Femi (think, thinks) too much of himself.
7. My brothers (prefer, prefers) reading to writing.
8. Martin (knows, know) exactly what to do.
9. Walter (is, are) good at motivating his employees.

Exercise E

Write these sentences using "have" or "has" in the blank spaces.

1. The sofa — six cushions.
2. Irene and her husband — a joint account.
3. The governor's position — been reinforced following his successful visit to the United States of America.
4. Wilson certainly — a just claim to the money.
5. I — got two days off this week.
6. Some directors — to share an office.
7. The ex-convict — renounced her old criminal way of life.

8. Believers — a duty to win souls.
9. This department — been the Cinderella of this ministry for far too long.
10. The old man's health — declined recently.
11. Angela — finished her assignment.
12. — you seen my new pair of shoes?
13. That young man — written an interesting book.
14. They — sold their house.
15. — you read the book on subject-verb agreement?
16. The police — arrested an innocent man.
17. We — axed 80 per cent of our staff.
18. The professors — arrived.
19. Juliet — a very good figure.
20. I — no idea how he came here.
21. He — an ulterior motive in offering to help her.
22. You — to go.

Exercise F

Write these sentences using either "do" or "does" in each of the blank spaces.

1. — you mind talking a little louder?
2. Make sure you — exactly what your parents want.
3. Roland — not like swimming.
4. Such things — not occur here.
5. — he speak Spanish?
6. Good things — not come easy.
7. How — you do?
8. — you understand what I am saying?
9. — you take sugar?
10. — she live here?

Exercise G

Conjugate each of these verbs in the present tense of the active voice.

1. dive
2. hear
3. climb
4. swim

5. say
6. jump
7. dig
8. walk
9. draw
10. want

Exercise H

Underline the correct verb in each of the following sentences.

1. Prayer (work, works).
2. He (respects, respect) his elders.
3. I (trust, trusts) God.
4. The dog (belongs, belong) to my uncle.
5. Chioma (needs, need) a new uniform.
6. Harmony (plays, play) basketball very well.
7. Justice Kate (hates, hate) cats.
8. I (give, gives) God all the glory.
9. I (need, needs) to think big.
10. Wolves (live, lives) and hunt in groups.

Exercise I

Copy the following sentences, supplying the verb that agrees with the subject.

1. My sister or nanny (is, are) feeding my baby.
2. The seven o'clock news (are, is) over.
3. Part of the students (has, have) finished their examinations.
4. Fifteen inches (is, are) the exact measurement.
5. It is not the nurses but the doctor who (is, are) leaving the clinic.
6. One of the boxers (is, are) unconscious.
7. Half of the doughnut (is, are) burnt.
8. Everyone (is, are) willing to attend the wedding.
9. Neither the principal nor the students (has, have) arrived.
10. Either the officers or the director (has, have) gone home.
11. Akpan, as well as Chike, (drive, drives) recklessly.
12. Everybody (wants, want) to see the painting.
13. The plumber, as well as his apprentice, (are, is) repairing the water pipes.

14. Patience, together with humility, (is, are) a fruit of the Spirit.
15. One of the lawyers (has, have) lost the case.
16. One of my colleagues (is, are) getting married next week.
17. Either of the girls (have, has) gone to school.
18. Each of the men (is, are) resting.
19. Both (are, is) to sweep the compound.
20. Many of the students (is, are) doing well.
21. It is not the girls but their auntie who (is, are) mopping the floor.
22. Macdons (is, are) a fast food restaurant with a restful atmosphere.
23. The pliers (is, are) very expensive.
24. The pair of scissors (is, are) blunt.
25. *Rainbows Are for Lovers* (is, are) an interesting book by Okedu Wale.
26. Here (is, are) my parents.
27. I (don't, doesn't) like monkeys.
28. It is not the students but their teacher who (is, are) writing.

ANSWERS

Exercise A

1. have
2. do not
3. are
4. looks
5. think
6. sells
7. speaks
8. prefer
9. occupies
10. enjoys
11. is
12. are

Exercise B

1. Ada <u>sings</u> well.
2. Benice always <u>makes</u> me laugh.
3. Patricia and Onyeka <u>obey</u> their parents.
4. I never <u>listen</u> to gossip.
5. The athletes <u>swim</u> very well.
6. Commercial buses to Agbor <u>run</u> every half hour.
7. I <u>stand</u> upon the word of God.
8. Highly qualified engineers <u>seek</u> employment.
9. Utomi's brothers <u>love</u> him very much.
10. Roseline <u>cares</u> for her children.
11. I <u>appreciate</u> your kind offer.
12. I <u>give</u> you twenty-four hours to explain why disciplinary action should not be taken against you.

Exercise C

1. is
2. do
3. say
4. lack
5. has
6. write
7. admire
8. charms

Exercise D

1. likes
2. is
3. has
4. is
5. are
6. thinks
7. prefer
8. knows
9. is

Exercise E

1. has
2. have
3. has
4. has
5. have
6. have
7. has
8. have
9. has
10. has
11. has

12. Have
13. has
14. have
15. Have
16. have
17. have
18. have
19. has
20. have
21. has
22. have

Exercise F

1. Do
2. do
3. does
4. do
5. Does

6. do
7. do
8. Do
9. Do
10. Does

Exercise G

Dive

Persons	Singular	Plural
First person	I dive	We dive
Second person	You dive	You dive
Third person	He dives, She dives, It dives	They dive

Hear

Persons	Singular	Plural
First person	I hear	We hear
Second person	You hear	You hear
Third person	He hears, She hears, It hears	They hear

Climb

Persons	Singular	Plural
First person	I climb	We climb
Second person	You climb	You climb
Third person	He climbs, She climbs, It climbs	They climb

Swim

Persons	Singular	Plural
First person	I swim	We swim
Second person	You swim	You swim
Third person	He swims, She swims, It swims	They swim

Say

Persons	Singular	Plural
First person	I say	We say
Second person	You say	You say
Third person	He says, She says, It says	They say

Dig

Persons	Singular	Plural
First person	I dig	We dig
Second person	You dig	You dig
Third person	He digs, She digs, It digs	They dig

Walk

Person	Singular	Plural
First person	I walk	We walk
Second person	You walk	You walk
Third person	He walks, She walks, It walks	They walk

Draw

Persons	Singular	Plural
First person	I draw	We draw
Second person	You draw	You draw
Third person	He draws, She draws, It draws	They draw

Want

Persons	Singular	Plural
First person	I want	We want
Second person	You want	You want
Third person	He wants, She wants, It wants	They want

Exercise H

1. works
2. respects
3. trust
4. belongs
5. needs

6. plays
7. hates
8. give
9. need
10. live

Exercise I

1. is
2. is
3. have
4. is
5. is
6. is
7. is
8. is
9. have
10. has
11. drives
12. wants
13. is
14. is

15. has
16. is
17. has
18. is
19. are
20. are
21. is
22. is
23. are
24. is
25. is
26. are
27. don't
28. is

REFERENCES

Barber, Katherine, ed. *The Canadian Oxford Dictionary.* Canada: Oxford University Press, 1998.

Barber, Katherine, et al. *Oxford Canadian Dictionary of Current English.* Canada: Oxford University Press, 2005.

Brown, Lesley, ed. *The New Shorter Oxford English Dictionary.* New York: Oxford University Press, 1993.

Hornby, Albert Sydney. *Oxford Advanced Learner's Dictionary.* Britain: Oxford University Press, 2005.

Merriam-Webster. *Merriam-Webster's Dictionary of Basic English.* Springfield, Massachusetts: Merriam-Webster, 2009.

Robbins, Lara M. *Grammar and Style at Your Fingertips.* Indianapolis: Penguin, 2007.

Shane, Harold G., Florence K. Ferris, and Edward E. Keener. *Using Good English.* Republic of the Philippines: Laidlaw Brothers, 1956.

Stevenson, Angus, and Maurice Waite, eds. *Concise Oxford English Dictionary.* New York: Oxford University Press, 2011.